Colonial Williamsburg
The First 75 Years

By Mary Miley Theobald

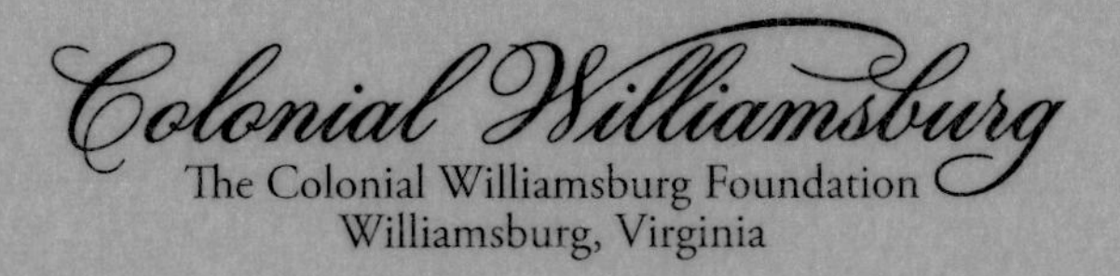

Colonial Williamsburg
The First 75 Years

By Mary Miley Theobald

Colonial Williamsburg
The Colonial Williamsburg Foundation
Williamsburg, Virginia

SEMPER EADEM

PROLOGUE

Williamsburg was seventy-five years old when Virginia's colonial leaders met to defy the mightiest military power in the world. Risking their lives, their fortunes, and their sacred honor, they elected delegates to the first Continental Congress and set themselves on the perilous road to independence. This is the Williamsburg we see today, a city vibrant with the voices of history, a city that honors those men and women of all colors, occupations, and classes who sacrificed their present that the future might live free.

Colonial Williamsburg is seventy-five years old this year. We celebrate this landmark with a nod to the past and a vision of the future, confident that Colonial Williamsburg will continue as a symbol of our nation's finest ideals for as long as those ideals endure.

The Governor's Palace, view from the formal gardens.

Dr. W. A. R. Goodwin (*above*) and with John D. Rockefeller, Jr. (*above right*).

THE MINISTER AND THE PHILANTHROPIST

"Late on a moonlight night you can see . . ."

It was 1926. The Roaring Twenties. The Jazz Age. Prohibition, the Charleston, silent movies. Richard E. Byrd flew over the North Pole, Henry Ford introduced the forty-hour work week, President Calvin Coolidge pledged to reduce taxes . . . and John D. Rockefeller, Jr., only son of America's first billionaire, made his first trip to Williamsburg.

A business trip to Hampton Institute turned into a family holiday—his wife, Abby, and three of their five sons had come along to see the old colonial capitals of Williamsburg and Jamestown and the battlefield at Yorktown. In Williamsburg, Rockefeller met with Dr. W. A. R. Goodwin, rector of Bruton Parish Church and professor of philosophy at the College of William and Mary. The two men had been introduced two years earlier in New York where they found they had something in common: both were members of Phi Beta Kappa, America's oldest honor society. They shared something else far more significant—a passion for America's proud heritage—but they didn't know that yet.

The Episcopal minister hoped to infect the philanthropist with preservation fever. For twenty years, Goodwin had dreamed of restoring Virginia's colonial capital to its former glory, creating a town where history would speak directly to modern Americans, where the future would draw inspiration from the past. "I am convinced," he wrote, "that from an historical point of view this is the greatest teaching opportunity which exists in America."

Once upon a time, Williamsburg had been the capital of Great Britain's largest, wealthiest, and most populous mainland colony. Nourished by fertile Virginia soil, the ideals of individual liberty, self-government, and religious freedom took root. Here British colonists such as George Washington, Thomas Jefferson, Patrick Henry, James Madison, Peyton Randolph, George Wythe, and ordinary men and women became Americans. Here they imagined and worked out and fought for a new sort of nation with a government of the people, by the people, and for the people. The Revolutionary War came late to Williamsburg but it came, in the form of occupations by first the British and then the American and French armies massing for battle in nearby Yorktown, the great battle of 1781 that would end British rule in the thirteen colonies. Forty-three years later, an aging Lafayette returned to Williamsburg to visit the town where he and Washington had headquartered and to accept the thanks of a grateful people.

Toward the war's end, Williamsburg's importance began to decline. When the General Assembly moved the capital to Richmond in 1780, the newspaper, several merchants, and many townspeople followed. Just five years later, a traveler from New England would describe Williamsburg as "beautiful" but "decaying." By 1800, it had lost about a third of its prewar population of 1,880 souls.

But Williamsburg refused to wither away. It was still the county seat and home to the state's respected public mental hospital, oldest college, and U. S. district court. St. George Tucker, a distinguished Williamsburg resident, described the town after the Revolution as having respectable inhabitants and an agreeable, friendly society. By the middle of the nineteenth century, Williamsburg's population had begun to grow again. It survived the occupation by Union forces during the Civil War and the poverty of Reconstruction. Ultimately, Williamsburg's very obscurity was what preserved it for future generations, for in this small market town, there was little reason to knock down old buildings and replace them with new ones.

Looking east on Duke of Gloucester Street around 1890.

12/7/26

Form 1204

CLASS OF SERVICE	SYMBOL
TELEGRAM	
DAY LETTER	BLUE
NIGHT MESSAGE	NITE
NIGHT LETTER	N L

If none of these three symbols appears after the check (number of words) this is a telegram. Otherwise its character is indicated by the symbol appearing after the check.

WESTERN UNION TELEGRAM

NEWCOMB CARLTON, PRESIDENT GEORGE W. E. ATKINS, FIRST VICE-PRESIDENT

CLASS OF SERVICE	SYMBOL
TELEGRAM	
DAY LETTER	BLUE
NIGHT MESSAGE	NITE
NIGHT LETTER	N L

If none of these three symbols appears after the check (number of words) this is a telegram. Otherwise its character is indicated by the symbol appearing after the check.

The filing time as shown in the date line on full-rate telegrams and day letters, and the time of receipt at destination as shown on all messages, is STANDARD TIME.

Received at
18RDW 23

MD NEW YORK NY 1051A DEC 7

DR W A R GOODWIN

COLLEGE OF WILLIAM AND MARY WILLIAMSBURG VA

AUTHORIZE PURCHASE OF ANTIQUE REFERRED TO IN YOUR LONG LETTER OF DECEMBER FOURTH AT EIGHT ON BASIS OUTLINED IN SHORTER LETTER SAME DATE

DAVIDS FATHER

1128 AM

ARCHIVES RECORD COPY COLONIAL WILLIAMSBURG

The Restoration really began with this coded telegram from Mr. Rockefeller to Dr. Goodwin, instructing him to purchase the Paradise House (*above*). To preserve his anonymity, Rockefeller signed the telegram "David's father," knowing that the minister would remember meeting his lively youngest son. The original Courthouse as it appeared during the 1920s (*right*). Just beyond the Courthouse sits the only hotel in town. It was later replaced by Chowning's Tavern.

Dr. Goodwin was more than a dreamer. Within the limitations of his income, he had made modest progress toward his goal by raising enough money to restore the interior of historic Bruton Parish Church and he was working to save one important colonial house—the home of George Wythe—from demolition. By 1926, he felt a sense of urgency. At fifty-six, he was no longer a young man. The town's colonial-era buildings were dilapidated. The Wythe House, home of a signer of the Declaration of Independence, stood abandoned, its doors and windows gaping like sightless eyes. The Governor's Palace and the old Capitol building had already burned down; others were not far behind them in succumbing to the ravages of time.

Dr. Goodwin understood the power of Williamsburg's past. He was convinced that anyone who walked in the footsteps of the Founding Fathers and surrendered to imagination could not help but absorb his vision. During the tour he gave the Rockefeller family, he captured the attention of the three boys like the Pied Piper, bringing to life the Revolutionary heroes they knew only from schoolbooks. "[Rockefeller's] interest was awakened," said Dr. Goodwin, hardly daring to hope.

On November 27 of that same year, Rockefeller made a second trip to Williamsburg. The occasion was the 150th anniversary celebration of the Phi Beta Kappa Society, founded at the College of William and Mary in 1776. He and Dr. Goodwin took the opportunity to tour Williamsburg once again. Some say that Mr. Rockefeller wandered off alone for awhile to ponder the possibilities. Before the banquet ended that evening, Rockefeller had authorized Dr. Goodwin to hire an architect. Ten days later, he sent word to buy the Paradise House, an eighteenth-century property that was on the market. Colonial Williamsburg had begun.

"It is my desire and purpose to carry out this enterprise completely and entirely," wrote Rockefeller a year later. "The purpose of this undertaking is to restore Williamsburg, so far as it may be possible, to what it was in the old colonial days and to make it a great center for historical study and inspiration." The minister's dream of saving America's past for her future was becoming a reality.

Prentis Store is the oldest surviving commercial building in Williamsburg. Built around 1740, it was being used as a gas station when the Restoration acquired it.

THE BEGINNING

"My gawd they've sold the town!"

Dr. Goodwin lost no time buying up historic property. Of course, such purchases were impossible on a minister's salary and everyone knew that he had finally found a benefactor, but who was it? Rockefeller had insisted that his role be kept confidential for the time being, and, amazingly, the secret held fast for almost two years. Some people suspected Henry Ford, who had visited Williamsburg twice (and would go on to develop his own historic Greenfield Village near Detroit); others speculated that financier J. P. Morgan, Jr., was providing the funds. Finally, at a town meeting in June 1928, Dr. Goodwin publicly revealed the name of the man responsible for Williamsburg's imminent renaissance. By then, Mr. Rockefeller had already spent three million dollars (the equivalent of ten times that amount today).

The Boston architectural firm of Perry, Shaw and Hepburn was engaged to handle the ambitious restoration project. Overnight, it seemed, "the town that time forgot" collided with modernity. Streets were torn up, telephone poles torn down, many Victorian buildings torn out, new additions torn off. Electricians buried unsightly telephone and electric lines. Colonial-era structures—some so decayed that the next decent gust of wind might have toppled them—were identified and marked for preservation. The sleepy southern town described by one turn-of-the-century resident as "dead as Pompeii" had come wide awake.

But the science of historic preservation was new and its practitioners had to grope their way along, collecting countless physical measurements from surviving colonial buildings up and down the Atlantic coast. From privies to palaces, they gathered photographs, made

measurements, and took notes on every imaginable structural detail, pursuing each scrap of evidence with the zeal of Sherlock Holmes. Archaeologists painstakingly sifted through tons of Williamsburg earth to uncover long-buried foundations and millions of artifacts, each one a clue to the appearance of a building or the lifestyle of its inhabitants. Historians combed libraries in Europe and America for eighteenth-century letters, books, newspapers, ship manifests, wills, inventories, insurance policies, and other historical records. The effort, which continues to this day, uncovered a treasure trove of information that guided the restoration of the eighty-eight original structures still standing in the designated Historic Area and the reconstruction of hundreds of others that had long since disappeared.

Just as modern prosperity had once bypassed Williamsburg, so now did the Great Depression. While the rest of America struggled through a decade of unprecedented hardship, Williamsburg during the 1930s was a beehive swarming with busy workers.

Suitable building materials were at a premium. After a futile search for authentic-looking and commercially available bricks, Restoration officials threw up their hands and started their own brickyard. A new sort of fireproof shingle that mimicked weathered wood was developed for many roofs. A centuries-old English glass manufacturer provided some windowpanes just like the originals. Colonial paint colors were determined by scrapings, and later by more accurate chemical analysis. The stone in the floor of the original House of Burgesses was traced to a quarry in England and the same stone was imported for its reconstruction.

Many Williamsburg property owners sold their homes to the Williamsburg Holding Company during those first years. Some who owned eighteenth-century buildings were offered a "life tenancy" to induce them to sell. These families were able to sell their homes, watch them be restored and modernized, then move back in to live rent free for the remainder of their lives or their children's lives. Other restored or reconstructed buildings were rented to employees. Business owners were encouraged to move to new quarters provided in the designated "business block" (today known as Merchants Square) that was planned at the college end of the street where no original buildings were believed to have survived. A new

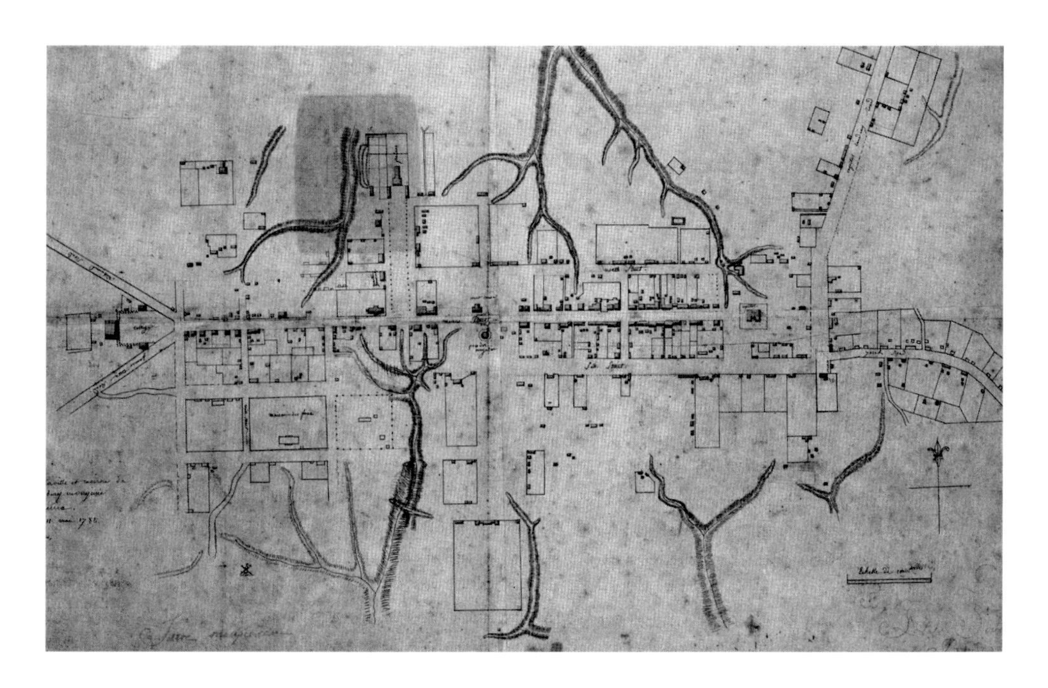

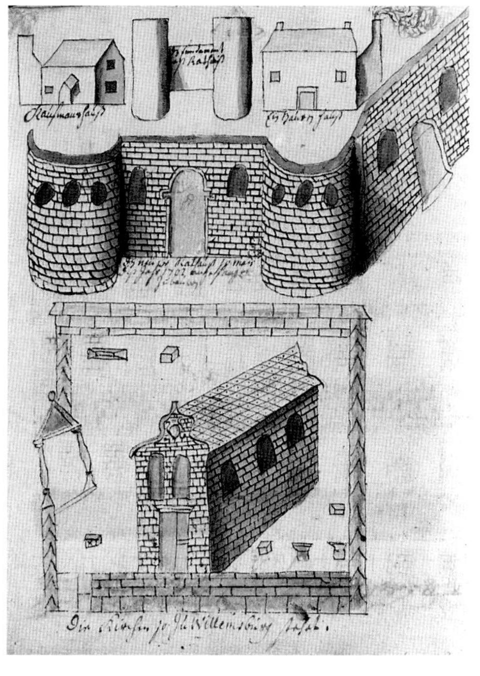

Clockwise from top: The "Frenchman's Map," The Bodleian Plate, and a drawing by Swiss traveler Francis Louis Michel were among the important visual records that guided Restoration architects. Courtesy of Swem Library, College of William and Mary ("Frenchman's Map") and Burgerbibliothek Bern (Michel drawings).

public school was built to allow the two old ones sitting atop the Palace foundations to be torn down. A modern courthouse was presented to the city in exchange for the 1770 courthouse on Market Square. An up-to-date fire station just outside the Historic Area replaced the old one.

Recognizing that they could not lead the Restoration effort without assistance, Dr. Goodwin and John D. Rockefeller, Jr., brought in Colonel Arthur Woods, Kenneth Chorley, and the eldest Rockefeller son, John D. 3rd, to serve in executive positions in Colonial Williamsburg, Inc., and on the board of trustees. Locally, Vernon M. Geddy, Sr., a Williamsburg lawyer, served as the organization's first president and continued as a resident executive vice president. Like the producers and directors who take a movie from script to screen, this first-generation leadership took the Williamsburg dream from historical record into the streets as a living museum.

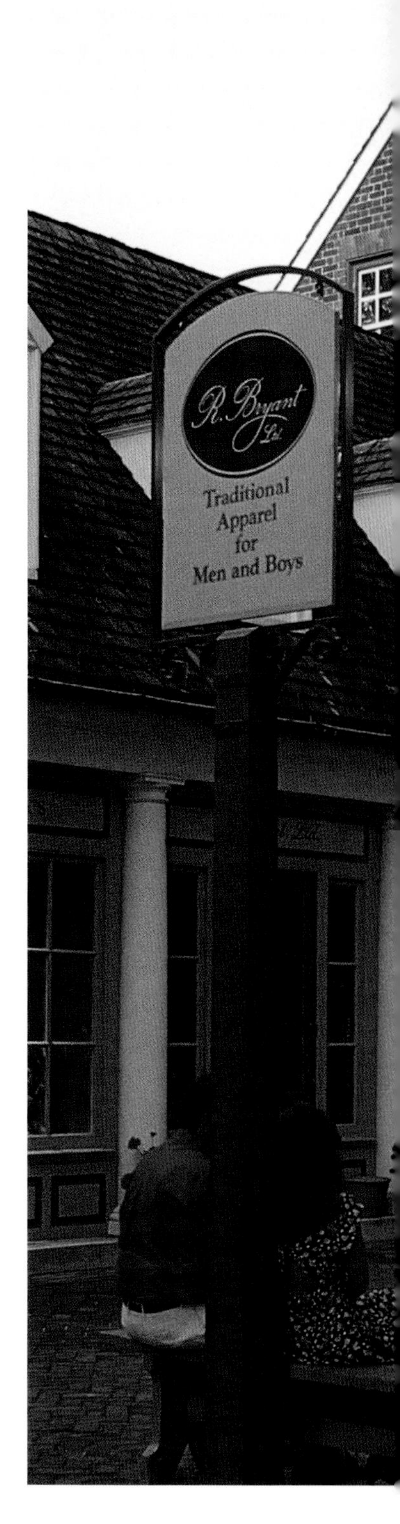

Merchants Square in the days before the Restoration (*above*) and today (*right*).

THE

President Franklin D. Roosevelt visited Colonial Williamsburg in 1934 (*above*). The Capitol building was reconstructed on its original site (*right*).

LAYING THE FOUNDATIONS

"The most historic avenue in all America"

Buildings sprouted faster than daffodils in the warm winter sun. In 1932, the Raleigh Tavern, the first exhibition building to be reconstructed on its original foundations, began offering tours to the public for forty cents. The Capitol and the Governor's Palace opened their doors two years later. Restored buildings were completed at a dizzying pace throughout the thirties, some for exhibition such as the Courthouse of 1770, the Public Gaol, the Paradise House, and the George Wythe House; most for residential use.

From the outset, Colonial Williamsburg worked closely with two institutions, the College of William and Mary, a state-supported university chartered in 1693, and Bruton Parish Church, an Episcopal church in continuous use since 1715. Rockefeller was committed to the meticulous restoration of as many eighteenth-century buildings in Williamsburg's Historic Area as possible, including the three eighteenth-century buildings that formed the heart of the college—the Wren Building, the President's House, and the Brafferton—and Bruton Parish Church.

Gardens and greens that surrounded the historic structures were vital to the town's overall appearance. Rockefeller hired noted landscape architect Arthur Shurcliff, then president of the American Society of Landscape Architects, to take the lead in the town's outdoor restoration. Shurcliff and his crews would research and reestablish Governor Francis Nicholson's town plan of 1699, re-creating its expansive greens and vistas and replanting as accurately as possible its formal gardens, orchards, flower gardens, vegetable and herb gardens, and pastures.

JAMES
JEWELLER

Inventory studies determined that the refurbished room (*above*) should be the dining room at the Peyton Randolph House, not the parlor as was long thought (*right*).

Empty buildings, no matter how carefully restored, could not portray the essence of eighteenth-century life. In 1931, Colonial Williamsburg hired James Cogar as its first professional curator to research, purchase, and install antiques in the buildings scheduled for exhibition. He began vigorously collecting period pieces, more than enough to ensure that the first exhibition buildings opened fully furnished. The collecting emphasis during the Cogar years—and those of his successor, John Graham—was on the rare and beautiful rather than the typical, and many of the treasures they acquired are displayed today in the DeWitt Wallace Decorative Arts Museum. Later, as curator Graham Hood took charge, the focus shifted and interiors came to reflect more accurately their eighteenth-century appearance.

By 1934, after eight years of work, the removal of four hundred modern structures, and the restoration or reconstruction of one hundred fifty early buildings, Colonial Williamsburg was ready for its formal debut. President Franklin D. Roosevelt came to dedicate the town with a speech. Motoring down Duke of Gloucester Street as American flags unfurled inspired him to call it "the most historic avenue in all America." Thirty-one thousand visitors flocked to the colonial town that first year.

The seeds of Colonial Williamsburg's most enduring programs were planted during the thirties. Evening concerts at the Governor's Palace grew into a strong music program. The Christmas wreaths and candlelight illuminations ripened into an old-fashioned holiday celebration and sparked a resurgence of enthusiasm for natural materials and homemade decorations. A handful of costumed "hostesses" and three craftsmen started what would become the largest, most carefully researched interpretive effort in America. Half a dozen cozy rooms in the Raleigh Hotel (Market Square Tavern today) evolved into a hotel division with mutiple hotels and conference facilities. A pioneering effort at making reproductions became the oldest comprehensive museum reproductions program in the country.

Magazines went wild for Williamsburg. *National Geographic, House & Garden,* and several architectural journals were the first to appear with extensive features extolling the marvels of the Restoration. They, along with *House Beautiful, The Magazine Antiques, Reader's Digest,* and countless others, have devoted thousands of pages over the years to Colonial Williamsburg's gardens, buildings, house plans, furnishings, and reproductions program. Predictably, each article encourages a new generation of Americans to make the pilgrimage to Williamsburg.

Wreaths trimmed with fresh fruit and candles glowing in the windows have been the hallmarks of a Williamsburg Christmas since the early years of the Restoration. The natural decorations appealed to a town trying to create new traditions and sparked a nation-wide enthusiasm for homemade decorations of materials from nature.

Even before the Historic Area's official opening in 1934, curious Americans had started arriving in Williamsburg. In the beginning, it was supposed that people would come to the Restored Area, absorb its inspiring message, then go on their way. The notion of accommodating a few of them overnight in old-style inns seemed reasonable. But it was soon evident that Williamsburg would draw far more visitors than expected, and that more overnight accommodations would be required. The town had a few guesthouses (today we would call them bed-and-breakfasts). The only hotel, a small Victorian-era structure across from the Magazine, was destined for the wrecking ball. Chowning's Tavern was reconstructed in its place and opened in 1941.

Hastily, Colonial Williamsburg officials set out to design and construct a "magnificent hostelry" just outside Historic Area boundaries. The Williamsburg Inn, modeled after the hot mineral spring resorts of antebellum Virginia, opened its doors in 1937. Unsurpassed at the time in comfort and luxury, the Inn was without peer among American hotels. The first in the country to have central air-conditioning in the public areas and in some of its sixty-one guest rooms, it boasted private bathrooms with ice water taps in every room. Noted interior designer Susan Higginson Nash decorated the rooms and public spaces in Regency-era style tempered with the warmth of an English country house.

Fears that Inn rooms would stand vacant most of the year proved unfounded—so much so that two years later, the Williamsburg Lodge was added. In 1938, the Inn delighted visitors by opening up two restored original buildings, the Quarter and the Orrell House, for overnight accommodations. From that modest beginning grew today's Colonial Houses program, providing guests with the opportunity to spend the night in one of twenty-eight unique Historic Area buildings. The 350th anniversary of the Jamestown settlement brought about a third hotel in 1957, the Motor House, later renamed

The Williamsburg Inn.

the Woodlands. A fourth, the Governor's Inn, was added in 1985.

Colonial Williamsburg was always a larger undertaking than anyone realized at the outset. Nothing on this scale had ever been attempted. True, a number of important shrines had been restored individually, and all over America, people—women's groups in particular—were increasingly aware of the need for preserving historic buildings, but no one had dared to take on an entire town. Rockefeller understood—as few others did—that saving a few scattered buildings in modern context could never convey an accurate picture of colonial life. He wanted nothing less than to rescue the colonial era from the history textbooks.

At the end of the astonishingly productive decade of the 1930s, the heart of the Restoration passed away. Dr. W. A. R. Goodwin lived long enough to see his greatest dream accomplished. Just as Mr. Rockefeller's five sons carried on his personal commitment to Colonial Williamsburg, Dr. Goodwin's son Rutherfoord and others of his family continued his work.

The emphasis during the early years was naturally on the physical restoration of the town: the buildings, the streets, the gardens, and the buffer zones that shielded the Historic Area from modern intrusions. However, no one lost sight of the ultimate goal, the larger and more elusive preservation of the fundamental concepts of freedom and responsibility that supported the creation of our country. Once the stage was set, it was time to bring on the players.

To keep modern intrusions out of sight, Dr. Goodwin conceived a plan most thought outrageous. He would divert traffic through a tunnel underneath the city. Rockefeller was flabbergasted: "I never heard of a crazier idea in my life." But the minister had lost none of his persuasive powers, and in 1940 Goodwin's tunnel was constructed and maintained by the National Park Service.

"I have high hopes for the future of Restored Williamsburg. . . . May you find as much pleasure, in carrying on the Restoration, as I have had in developing it, and may this restored city ever stand as a beacon light of freedom to the world."

BASSETT HALL

The Rockefellers needed a permanent base in Williamsburg from which to oversee the Restoration. At Dr. Goodwin's recommendation, John, Jr., purchased Bassett Hall, an eighteenth-century dwelling located at the edge of the Historic Area, for his family's use. After the house was renovated and furnished in 1936, the Rockefellers moved in. For over forty years, family members came often to visit Williamsburg and stay at this comfortable home. In 1979, they donated the building and all its furnishings, artwork, and land to Colonial Williamsburg. When the house opened to the public the next year, it looked substantially as it had appeared in the 1930s when Mrs. Rockefeller filled it with examples of American folk art, antiques, and comfortable furniture. A major renovation project of the house and gardens is tentatively scheduled for completion in 2002.

The Rockefellers usually visited Williamsburg in the spring and fall, staying at Bassett Hall for about six weeks at a time. It was Mrs. Rockefeller's favorite home.

LIFE ON THE SCENE

"People who used to live here in the long gone years . . ."

If Colonial Williamsburg were to be populated with patriots, soldiers, slaves, and craftsmen, they would have to be trained in historical interpretation and clothed from the toes up. Tour guides, originally called hostesses, came first to the historic Williamsburg stage. On the occasion of President Roosevelt's visit in 1934, six local ladies selected for their southern charm and gracious manners greeted him, splendidly dressed in yards of colorful, crisp fabric draped over wide hoops. Life on the scene had begun.

Over the next few months, the town blossomed like a meadow with wildflowers as janitors, coachmen, laundry workers, and the public gaoler were added to the list of costumed employees. Within two years, fifty-three men and women worked in costume, keeping two seamstresses and two laundresses busy. As always, the password was authenticity. Historians studied antique clothing, prints, portraits, and other records dealing with eighteenth-century dress in America and in Europe before translating their finds into clothing reproductions.

Located at first in the Governor's Palace stables, the seamstresses conducted some of their hand sewing in front of the public and laundresses hung wet clothing on lines to dry and pressed the garments with flatirons. Practical considerations and the need for more space moved the operation to quarters above the Millinery Shop and out of public view.

Shortly before the United States entered World War II, Chowning's Tavern opened,

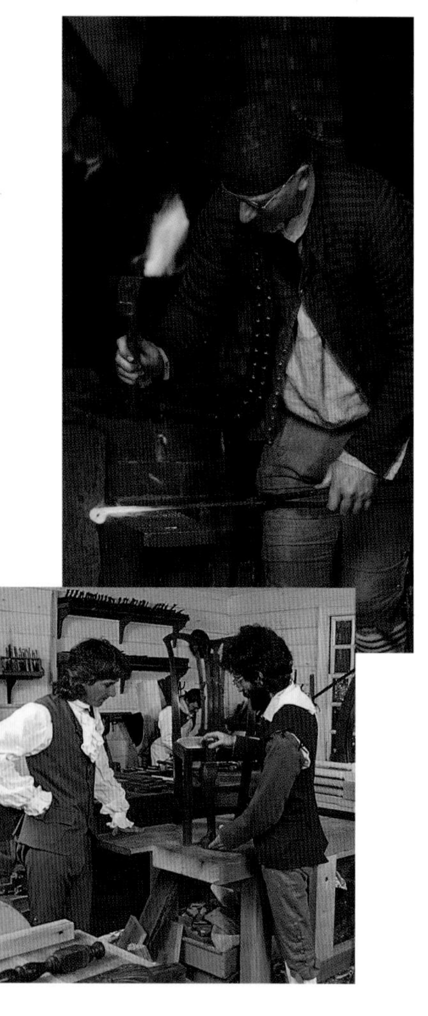

staffed with waiters dressed in eighteenth-century-style clothing. After the war, children joined the list of costumed personnel. So did maids, concert musicians, militiamen, and theater actors, bringing the total to five hundred, where it remained—give or take a few dozen—for decades. In 1956, the ladies of the hostess corps graciously made room for the first "host." The 1960s saw the extra wide side hoops (a feature of the 1740s style) replaced with more moderate bulges typical of the 1770s. Preparations for the 1976 U. S. Bicentennial crowds brought concerns about the cost of costuming so many additional employees. As an experiment, red, white, and blue polyester knit suits were ordered for the summer hostesses in 1973. Visitors were horrified. Costumes had become a Williamsburg icon. The tricolor polyesters skulked into the ragbag.

The first hostesses received minimal training. A list of historical facts, a book with a description of the antiques in each room, and a walk about the building were considered adequate preparation for guiding tours. In the 1940s, three hostesses were asked to start a training department and set up classes for new and existing employees. Former schoolteachers, the ladies brought a degree of professionalism to the training of costumed interpreters that endures to this day.

Nothing inserted life into Colonial Williamsburg better than the crafts demonstration program. Aside from the obvious educational value, it would add the "middling sort"—the middle class of hardworking craftsmen and -women so important to the country's survival—and it would rescue old-fashioned skills from extinction. In 1936, three trades were selected to form the program's nucleus: a blacksmith, a cabinetmaker, and a pewterer. The men worked in costume making products to sell to the public.

Like everything else, the program expanded over the years. The original three operations were joined by the Boot Shop, the Spinning and Weaving Shop, a candlemaker, and the Barber and Perukemaker's Shop where the work was merely discussed,

not demonstrated. World War II shut down all of them except the furniture shop. In the 1950s, the Apothecary, the Bookbindery, the Millinery Shop, the Printing Office, and the Silversmith Shop joined the lineup. The militia program, then considered part of the Crafts Department, started in 1959 as an occasional activity for the tradesmen.

The militia began asking a few men and high school boys to play fifes and drums during their musters. This ad hoc military music gained some permanence when George Carroll was hired to form a regular Fife and Drum Corps in 1960. After Carroll left, Colonial Williamsburg brought British drummer John Moon to town in the early 1970s to train the boys in military precision and historical music. Girls were admitted to the ranks in 1999. Today, there are eighty members in the Fife and Drum Corps, all between the ages of eight and eighteen.

When the sixties struck and the rest

of the country was casting dark glances at longhaired hippies, Colonial Williamsburg was the only place where a man with a ponytail had the full approval of the public and his employer. More women joined the Crafts Department, not always to do "women's work." It was not unusual for colonial women to work alongside their husbands in the family business, so authenticity and "women's lib" converged nicely. New trades included clockmaking, engraving, shingle making, gunsmithing, papermaking, harness and saddle making, basketweaving, coopering, paper marbling, wheel making, and hearth cooking.

In the 1970s, about one hundred fifty people were demonstrating thirty-six different trades. To make it easier for them to focus on demonstrating and interpreting, the sales part of the job was removed to two general stores, Tarpley's and Prentis. About this time, the term "craft" was replaced with the historically accurate "trade" and the professionals in Colonial Williamsburg's Historic Trades Department began to be called tradesmen.

Around 1935, several nineteenth-century carriages were purchased as a way to bring a bit of colonial atmosphere to the streets. At first, they were put to use transporting hostesses to and from work and delivering the mail, then in 1942, they started giving rides to visitors for fifty cents. Colonial Williamsburg took a serious look at its carriage program in the 1950s and started altering the old vehicles to eighteenth-century specifications. The active

manufacture and maintenance of wheels, carts, and wagons has been carried on at the Wheelwright's since 1975. Two new carriages have been ordered from an outside manufacturer: a traveling coach currently under construction should be delivered in 2002 and a town coach will follow.

With carriages and carts must come horses. Some were bought, others were rented as needed. So were a few sheep, and a cow here or there, until the 1970s, when a serious effort got underway to show animals in their proper settings. By then, the Williamsburg hallmark had been set in concrete: the animals had to be as authentic as possible. Only certain breeds would do, so in the 1980s, the Coach and Livestock Department began collecting and breeding rare domestic animals, many of which can trace their ancestry back to the 1700s.

Identifying and finding animals that accurately represent eighteenth-century livestock is complicated. Often, these breeds are on the critically endangered list and are difficult to obtain—witness the efforts taken in 1990 to acquire a flock of purebred English Leicester sheep all the way from the island of Tasmania. Milking Red Devon cattle and Canadian horses now populate Williamsburg's fields and paddocks and some old breeds of domesticated poultry scratch about inside fenced enclosures. The spring lambing, so popular with visitors, began in 1983. The livestock contribute to the colonial ambience in another way, by supplying milk, eggs, and wool for the domestic trades.

FOUR CENTURIES OF HISTORY AT CARTER'S GROVE

Through the generosity of the Rockefeller family, Carter's Grove plantation came into the Colonial Williamsburg fold in 1963. Carter's Grove made it possible to portray rural life, something that could not be done as readily within the city of Williamsburg. Until the 1980s, eighteenth-century plantation life was the focus of the interpretation. During those years, several factors combined to alter this perspective: the discovery of the remains of a seventeenth-century settlement on the property, the initiative for greater authenticity, and the desire to tell the important twentieth-century story of the Colonial Revival.

At the time of the Carter's Grove donation, no one knew that the remains of one of America's earliest settlements lay between the front door of the Georgian mansion and the James River. Preserved beneath the layer of dirt that had been plowed for four centuries were the postholes and artifacts of Martin's Hundred. During the 1970s and 1980s, this site was excavated by Colonial Williamsburg archaeologists and publicized by the National Geographic Society, which helped fund the work. Bit by bit, archaeologists uncovered fragments of weapons, tools, armor, and household artifacts that told the story of this small town's brief existence. Charred residue and skeletons testified to its destruction during the Powhatan uprising of 1622.

A schematic representation of part of the settlement was built, including the Wolstenholme Towne fort, store, barn, and domestic unit, to help visitors understand how the site looked originally. The Winthrop Rockefeller Archaeology Museum opened in 1991, displaying the artifacts and telling the story of Virginia's earliest colonists. A reception center with an orientation film and exhibitions prepares visitors for the site.

Archaeologists also uncovered evidence of eighteenth-century gardens at the base of the mansion's terraced slopes, an enclosed garden that has since been re-created with vegetables, herbs, and flowers appropriate to the period. Agricultural endeavors in the fields and orchards play an important part in the interpretation, as do animals from the rare breeds program. A meticulously reconstructed slave quarter represents the rudimentary quality of life of Virginia's many enslaved inhabitants.

Architects studied the mansion, which had been significantly altered early in the twentieth century according to the Colonial Revival style. Their decision to preserve this aspect of the house meant exhibiting the rooms as they looked in the 1930s when they were furnished with an assortment of seventeenth- to twentieth-century antiques and reproductions. A six-mile country road between the plantation and Williamsburg opened in 1981, thereby allowing visitors to enjoy the unspoiled landscape of bygone centuries.

THE WAR YEARS

"This visit made me realize [our] heritage"

The rapid growth of the Historic Area came to a halt with the onset of World War II. The year preceding Pearl Harbor had set a record with 210,000 visitors, but, with America at war, tourism evaporated. Gasoline was rationed, new tires were unavailable, and most men and many women were serving overseas or in war-related industries.

John D. Rockefeller, Jr., saw a wartime mission for Colonial Williamsburg. With government approval, he directed the Restoration to provide a field course in American history for servicemen and -women to help them understand the ideals they were fighting for. More than half a million soldiers and sailors training in Virginia visited Williamsburg as guests of Mr. Rockefeller.

Americans on the home front carried on to the best of their abilities "for the duration." Colonial Williamsburg remained minimally open for military visits, but lack of men and materials put most of the six craft demonstrations on hold. Chowning's Tavern closed, leaving only the Travis House to serve meals. Fabric to make costumes was unavailable. The blackout policy canceled the Christmas candles in the windows. The Williamsburg Inn and other hotel properties operated throughout the war with rooms that were reserved for officers of the armed forces and their families at $3.50 a night.

The Craft House shut its doors for lack of merchandise, boxes, and workers. Brass,

Mr. Rockefeller, who headed the committee that raised funds to finance USO activities around the world, turned space in Merchants Square into a large USO recreation center. Three generations of women came to know this building after the war as Binn's.

iron, tin, and other metals reserved for military use were no longer available for making candlesticks, wrought-iron bootscrapes, or pewter spoons. Manufacturers that had formerly produced silver hollowware now made radar parts, surgical instruments, and wind-speed indicators for battleships; textile producers set aside their chintzes for khaki; furniture manufacturers turned out airplane wings instead of cabriole legs.

Although the fighting ended in 1945, the shortages of materials, scarcity of labor, and soaring prices did not. While there could not be much progress in the way of new construction or restoration work, postwar initiatives included specialized tours for schoolchildren, the annual Garden Symposium, and Williamsburg's first golf course. By 1949, visitation had returned to prewar levels.

The octagon-shaped Magazine was constructed in 1715 to store the arms and ammunition sent by Great Britain for the defense of the colony. After the capital moved to Richmond in 1780, the building saw use as a market house, a Baptist church, a Confederate arsenal, a dancing school, and a livery stable before it was restored in 1935.

1950s, 1960s, and 1970s: The Six Appeals

"The greatest teaching opportunity which exists in America"

There are as many reasons to visit Colonial Williamsburg as there are people who visit. It was clear to Carl Humelsine, the Foundation's fourth president and later chairman of the board of trustees, that the attractions fell into six major categories. He called them "the Six Appeals." For nearly two decades, they provided the framework for interpretation at Colonial Williamsburg.

I. ARCHITECTURE AND TOWN PLANNING

Although the most intensive rebuilding period occurred before World War II, the restoration of Williamsburg is the proverbial never-ending story. The city's two hundred fiftieth anniversary in 1949 was celebrated with the opening of two new exhibition buildings, the Magazine and the Guardhouse. By the midcentury mark, Colonial Williamsburg had restored 82 of the 88 original buildings, reconstructed 341 on their original sites, and removed or torn down 616 modern structures—all for an expenditure of $50 million, or about $355 million today.

The three decades following 1950 brought dozens of newly restored or reconstructed buildings onto the scene, including several that were opened to the public: the Printing Office, Margaret Hunter Millinery Shop, Golden Ball Silversmith, Windmill, and Hay's

Cabinetmaking Shop. Two dining taverns, King's Arms and Christiana Campbell's, brought to three the number of restaurants within the Historic Area. With a grand burst of energy, five new exhibition buildings welcomed visitors in 1968: Wetherburn's Tavern, James Geddy House and Foundry, Peyton Randolph House, McKenzie Apothecary, and the Wren Building at the College of William and Mary.

To accommodate the rising tide of tourism and eliminate traffic congestion, buses began transporting guests about town in 1949. Tranquility was preserved when the streets within the Historic Area boundaries were closed to motor traffic during daylight hours, at first only during periods of peak tourism, later year-round. In 1957, a modern Information Center (later called the Visitor Center) some distance from the Historic Area replaced the old reception center near the Williamsburg Inn, providing the Historic Area with a welcoming front door and plentiful space for parking.

II. GARDENS AND GREENS

Some say Williamsburg's greatest triumph occurs outdoors. People whose interests lie down the garden path take pleasure in the distinctive landscape of colonial times. Formal pleasure gardens and kitchen gardens, enclosed and geometrically designed, were planted throughout the Historic Area during the early years of the Restoration. When subsequent research revealed that their manicured appearance was a bit overdone, a more relaxed standard was instituted. The list of authentic trees, bushes, plants, and flowers changes constantly as new research adds to or subtracts from what is known to have been grown in colonial Virginia. Today, a staff of seventy gardeners, horticulturists, and arborists using the latest environmentally sensitive methods actively maintains ninety acres of eighteenth-century gardens.

III. THE COLLECTION

From its first acquisition in 1928, the Department of Collections has grown to include more than sixty thousand objects. Most are British or American antiques acquired through purchase, gift, or bequest. Most are exhibited in the homes and public buildings of the Historic Area or in the galleries of the DeWitt Wallace Museum and the Abby Aldrich Rockefeller Folk Art Museum. From the larger-than-life Charles Willson Peale portrait of George Washington to the most insignificant straight pin, each object tells its own part of the complex story of early Virginia.

Curators, collectors, and connoisseurs delight in the annual learning fest known as the Antiques Forum. Every winter since 1949, the Antiques Forum has hosted lectures, discussions, special tours, and social gatherings that expand the boundaries of our knowledge of this fascinating field. That first year, the few dozen Forum participants gathered in the only space available: a Quonset hut next to the Williamsburg Lodge! Today, the well-appointed Williamsburg Lodge Conference Center welcomes five hundred participants to this popular annual symposium.

The first curators understood the need for proper care and conservation of the antiques. From the early years, furniture conservation was generally handled internally while paintings and paper objects usually traveled to outside specialists for restoration. Sometimes prominent conservators were brought in to take care of necessary repair and maintenance work. As the collection grew, so did the need for in-house expertise. In 1985, a separate Department of Conservation was created. Since that time, Colonial Williamsburg has become a leader in preventive conservation and a model for other institutions.

IV. HISTORICAL ARCHAEOLOGY

Archaeology came first at Colonial Williamsburg. Before anything could be reconstructed on or near its original foundations, those foundations had to be discovered and uncovered and the broken bits of history buried with them sorted and cataloged. During the first decades, the archaeology program was largely that: uncovering foundations. The science of archaeology was not yet advanced enough to "read" many of the underground clues, such as posthole evidence, and much went unnoticed. But as knowledge and technique improved,

Excavations at Wolstenholme Towne unearthed the story of this short-lived settlement and its destruction during the Powhatan uprising of 1622. Partial palisades mark the fort's outlines.

the amount of information gleaned from each site grew exponentially.

In 1957, the year of the three hundred fiftieth anniversary of the founding of Jamestown, an accelerated program of professional archaeology was launched under the direction of Ivor Noël Hume. Working with his wife, Audrey, also an archaeologist, he delved first into the sites of several trades shops and Wetherburn's Tavern, providing much-needed information about the furnishings and lifestyles of average Williamsburg residents. In 1976, the Noël Humes unexpectedly discovered the remains of Wolstenholme Towne, a seventeenth-century settlement long thought "lost," located near the Carter's Grove mansion. It took seven years—from 1976 to 1983—to open this Bicentennial birthday present, but when the excavations were completed, a new chapter of colonial history had been documented. To tell it properly meant re-creating the original fort's outlines, constructing in 1991 the Winthrop Rockefeller Archaeology Museum (named to honor his long interest in and support of Carter's Grove) to hold the artifacts, and publishing a mammoth report on Martin's Hundred in 2001.

Active archaeological sites always draw visitors like magnets. Everyone, it seems, loves a treasure hunt, especially when it reveals evidence that cannot be gleaned from written records. In recent years, excavations at the Peyton Randolph yard, the coffeehouse site near the Capitol, and the Hallam-Douglas Theater site near the Capitol have provided opportunities to watch and learn about this aspect of preservation research.

V. HISTORIC TRADES

Nothing conveys the stark difference between then and now as quickly as a tradesman working to accomplish by hand a task that takes almost no time with modern machinery. A vigorous Trades Department has long been an important part of Williamsburg's educational mission. Some ancient trades had languished over the centuries and needed a boost. Others had nearly died out and needed reviving. The only way that wigmaking, brickmaking, certain types of weaving, and the apothecary's trade could be resuscitated was with research and experimentation. Through the hard work and dedication of hundreds of tradesmen and women, Colonial Williamsburg has saved many historic handcrafts from extinction.

For forty years, each shop demonstrated its trade, interpreted it to the visitor, and made souvenirs to sell on the site. By the 1970s, the sales had become too great a burden, cutting into the educational mission, so two stores were opened in the Historic Area as outlets for handcrafted merchandise in 1973.

As the capital of Britain's largest and most populous mainland colony, Williamsburg was also the business center of Virginia. Shops and stores once lined Duke of Gloucester Street and the side streets, jostling with the taverns and ordinaries for position at the "better," more prosperous, end of town near the Capitol. In an effort to replicate this commercial bustle, seven more stores and shops were opened in their original locations. Each contributed to the fuller picture of eighteenth-century business: McKenzie Apothecary sold medicines, soaps, and other appropriate wares; the Golden Ball and the Geddy Shop dealt in gold and silver items, jewelry, and pewter. The Raleigh Tavern Bake Shop sold baked goods and cider. The Post Office mailed letters and sold paper, printed matter, and books while next door at M. Dubois Grocer there were packaged food items. In 1983, the general store that had belonged to John Greenhow two hundred years earlier reopened near Palace green. Shortly thereafter, the Geddy Shop changed to the historically more accurate Mary Dickinson Store. Everything from the merchandise assortment to its arrangement on the shelves is as authentic to the eighteenth century as possible.

VI. HISTORY AND HERITAGE

Taking history from textbook to the street is a task for a special sort of teacher. Whatever their specialties, Colonial Williamsburg's costumed interpreters are all history teachers. Whether they are guiding visitors through the Governor's Palace, herding flocks of schoolchildren past the pillory, or drilling with muskets in front of the Magazine, these hardy souls bring the past to life three hundred and sixty-five days of the year, through February ice storm or August heat wave. They form the front lines of the army of research historians, librarians, and program developers working behind the scenes to support every part of their presentations.

As America's first living history museum, Colonial Williamsburg blazed the trail into the uncharted world of public history. Exactly what history should Williamsburg be teaching? And how should its employees teach it? Rockefeller's motto, "That the future may learn from the past," provided the compass, but a new road map has had to be drawn for each generation.

Colonial Williamsburg's professional historians have long believed that the museum's education program should relate to the most important current issues before the American people. In the 1930s and 1940s, that meant self-sacrifice and patriotism. In the Cold War years, it meant the democratic ideals that opposed Communist totalitarianism. Delivering historical knowledge to the public—a process known as historical interpretation—was the realm of Edward P. Alexander, Williamsburg's leading educator from the end of World War II until 1972. Under his guidance, Williamsburg's historical interpreters developed principles, training programs, and teaching techniques that provided the public with sound historical information—plus a heavy dose of fun!

During one hectic three-week stretch in 1956, a thirty-seven-minute orientation movie was filmed at Williamsburg. *Williamsburg—The Story of a Patriot* with Jack Lord and a large professional cast was directed by Academy Award-winning screenwriter George Seaton and produced by Paramount Pictures for Colonial Williamsburg. Shown daily since 1957, this movie has provided thirty million visitors with a historical framework for their Williamsburg visit.

(*opposite*) Today's eighteenth-century dancing program traces its origins to the 1970s. About forty adult dancers and several students re-create Palace Balls and perform at various Historic Area evening events.

People of the past bring history to life. A reincarnated Patrick Henry gives his passionate Caesar-Brutus speech at the Capitol (*above*). Every July 4, the Declaration of Independence is proclaimed from the Courthouse steps (*right*).

1980S AND 1990S: VISIONS AND REVISIONS

"A beacon light of freedom to the world"

The fourth quarter of the twentieth century brought Bicentennial fever to Williamsburg. It seemed that every year saw the two hundredth anniversary of some significant event, starting with the buildup to the 1976 Bicentennial bash and continuing until 1999 when the country commemorated the two hundredth anniversary of the death of George Washington. Also in 1999, the city of Williamsburg observed its three hundredth birthday with a yearlong tercentennial celebration.

Extensive preparations were made for the record-breaking waves of visitors who were expected to flood into Williamsburg in 1976: a new ticket structure, many extra employees, new attractions (the wheelwright and the James Anderson House exhibitions), and special commemorative merchandise. But excessive media hype convinced many Americans to stay home that year, taking the air out of the Bicentennial balloon. Still, a record *was* set—1,280,000 visitors kept the Historic Area busy and the State Department's VIP program brought kings, prime ministers, and presidents from all over the world to join our nation's two hundredth birthday party.

In 1981, President Ronald Reagan and Vice President George Bush met with French President François Mitterrand in Williamsburg to celebrate the two hundredth anniversary of the Battle of Yorktown. They were joined by thousands of reenactors who gave a convincing

"May I just add a heartfelt thank you to the wonderful people of Williamsburg who have been so warm in their greeting to us, so gracious and so kind, and that have made this, in addition to a hard-working session, a distinct pleasure."—President Ronald Reagan

rendition of Revolutionary War camp life and warfare. Upon the invitation of Colonial Williamsburg President Charles R. Longsworth, Presidents Reagan and Mitterrand and heads of state representing Canada, the European Economic Community, the Federal Republic of Germany, Italy, Japan, and the United Kingdom returned for the Ninth Annual International Summit of Industrialized Nations, an event that captured the world's attention for three days in May 1983. The enormity of the Summit—the logistics, security, and transportation for eight heads of state, hundreds of political leaders, and thousands of members of the world press—caused Colonial Williamsburg to close the Historic Area to the public for the first time in history.

The last two decades of the twentieth century brought about the development of a comprehensive educational program that permeated every aspect of the visitor's experience at Colonial Williamsburg. By connecting the critical issues of the past to those that concern Americans today, the eighteenth century became less mysterious and the visitor's experience more meaningful.

A rededication to authenticity strengthened Colonial Williamsburg for the new millennium. This commitment manifested itself in two highly visible programs, a refurnishing of the entire Historic Area and a unique interpretive effort that shocked some and captivated most.

Chief Curator Graham Hood put spark to tinder when he embarked on a curatorial initiative to reevaluate the Historic Area interiors, building by building, starting with the Raleigh Tavern. During the forty years since the first exhibition rooms had been decorated, far more information had been uncovered, information that stubbornly pointed to a different "look" than the one in vogue two generations earlier. The romanticized Colonial Revival style of earlier years needed to give way to a more realistic version of colonial lifestyles.

Traditionalists howled as Hood trained his sights on the Governor's Palace. Never mind all the research proving the Palace had looked quite different—they *liked* it the way it was! The scholarship, however, was irrefutable, and when the redecorated Palace opened in 1981, even the critics had to admit its elegance had not suffered in the transition. Using the 1770

The Colonial Revival decorating style—a nostalgic, romanticized, and far more comfortable rendition of eighteenth-century interiors—dominated American interior decorating during the twentieth century and caused most historic houses to be restored in ways that matched modern expectations rather than actual lifestyles of the past. The Daphne Room at the Raleigh Tavern is shown decorated in the Colonial Revival style (*right*) and as it appears today (*above*).

inventory taken on the death of Governor Botetourt and his original account books, the curators turned detective. They carefully matched each of the sixteen thousand items on the inventory list with a corresponding object of the same origin, the same date, and the same appearance—and put it in the same room.

During the 1980s and 1990s, nearly every room in the Historic Area was researched, reanalyzed, and redecorated in this manner. In subtle ways, the curators tried to bring life to the silent rooms: a sock draped carelessly out of a drawer, playing cards and leftovers on the tavern table, toys scattered on the floor. One of the most striking changes was the addition of wallpaper—much of it brightly colored and boldly patterned—to walls where new research indicated it was appropriate.

The curatorial juggernaut was part and parcel to a broader reevaluation of the entire Historic Area. The architectural historians reviewed paint color analyses and found many buildings could be made more accurate with a fresh coat. The Geddy House exterior went

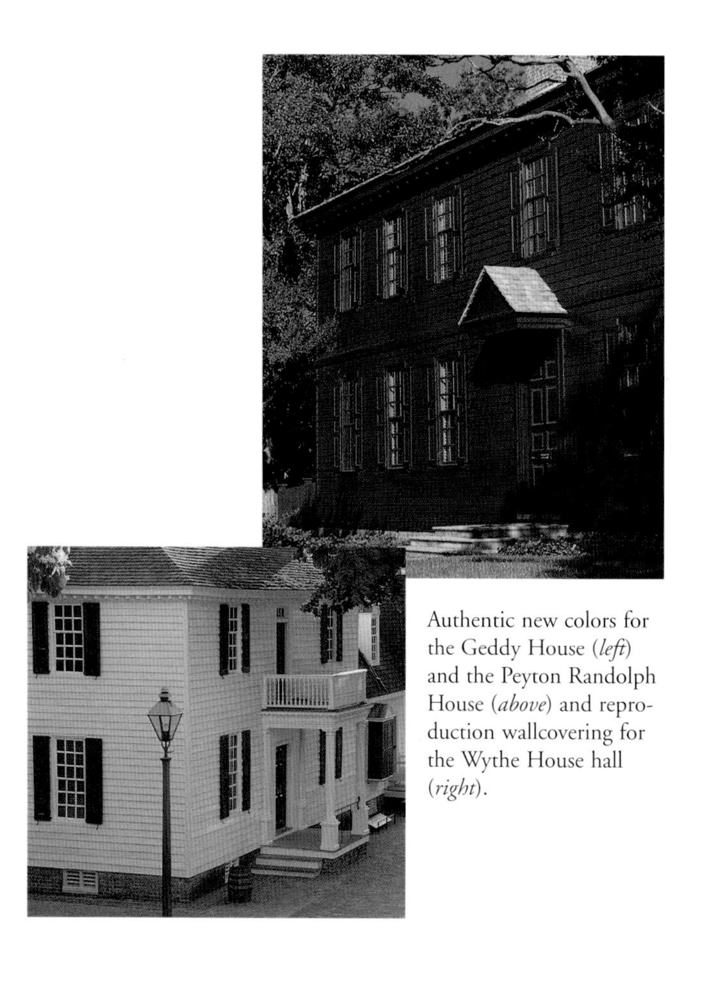

Authentic new colors for the Geddy House (*left*) and the Peyton Randolph House (*above*) and reproduction wallcovering for the Wythe House hall (*right*).

from blue-green to white, the Peyton Randolph from white to reddish brown. At the Costume Design Center, the standards of appearance were tightened. No longer would any plain black shoe or one's own modern eyeglasses suffice, and stays were recommended to give women the correct posture. Outdoors, horticulturists hunted down ancient varieties of fruit trees, such as Jefferson's favorite Albemarle Pippin or the Virginia Crab Apple, to use in orchards throughout the Historic Area. When research determined that plants like pyracantha and Osage orange were not appropriate to the time span, those specimens were removed from the Historic Area.

It was a time, too, for tackling important issues

Each year historical interpreters focused on a different aspect of the "Becoming Americans" main theme. "Redefining Family" (*above*) and "Taking Possession" (*right*) provide fresh insight into topics that are still highly relevant today.

that had long been ignored. Colonial Williamsburg interpreted political history very well indeed, but politics in the eighteenth century, by its very definition, excluded a large slice of the population pie. To portray the eighteenth century in a more authentic manner, African-Americans, women, Native Americans, children, and ordinary people needed greater visibility.

Visitors of the 1970s came to Williamsburg looking for the whole spectrum of eighteenth-century life. They wanted realism, color, action, and excitement, not a whitewashed, romanticized version of the past. They wanted stories about ordinary people—people like themselves—along with the famous names so they could see their own world and its place on the historic timeline. They expected conflict and controversy, the dramatic tension of everyday life during those dynamic formative years. And Colonial Williamsburg aimed to deliver.

A curriculum study group formed in 1977 created a new framework for interpretation that has, through several revisions, guided program development, research, and collecting ever since. Now called "Becoming Americans: Our Struggle to Be Both Free and Equal," the interpretive plan included everyone who had lived in eighteenth-century Williamsburg.

The main theme, "Becoming Americans," is presented through six story lines, each with its own particular places for visitors to go, its "People of the Past" to meet, and special programs to experience. Crafted with help from historical interpreters, historians, and curators, the latest outgrowth of this ambitious plan began in 1996. That year was devoted to "Choosing Revolution," which traces the beginnings of the new nation by exploring the complex decisions every Virginian faced as the colony moved toward independence.

For the five years following, visitors were introduced to the other interrelated story lines, "Redefining Family" in 1997 (exploring changing ideas of American family life as blacks, whites, and Native Americans interacted in the Virginia colony), "Freeing Religion" in 1998 (a survey of the religious life of the three cultures in Virginia and the changes that resulted in the guarantee of the free exercise of religion in Virginia and America), "Enslaving Virginia" in 1999 (the development of a racially based slave system in Virginia and its profound effect on the lives, fortunes, and values of blacks and whites), and "Taking Possession" in 2000 (the story of the colonists' quest for land and its effect on Native Americans, settlers, and the development of American values). In 2001, the sequence culminated with "Buying Respectability," an examination of rising consumerism at all levels of colonial society as learned social refinement and possession of fashionable items became widespread. "Becoming Americans" will continue to shape the visitor's experience at Colonial Williamsburg in the years to come.

"Affairs of the Heart," a pioneering program addressing interracial relationships, miscegenation, and the precarious nature of slave family life, began in 1994. The "Prime Time History Hour" debuted in 1995 as a family talk show about our pasts and our future. A host interviewed "guests" from the eighteenth century, then invited questions from the audience. The "Days in History" program added in 1999 highlights several important dates just prior to the Revolutionary War. Each day, the story concludes with an exciting five o'clock event.

"Buying Respectability" explores the consumer revolution of the eighteenth century.

In 2001, programs continued their focus on a specific year in history (1774), changing seasonally, with each day of the week devoted to a specific aspect of eighteenth-century life:

"court days" on the effect of law in everyday life, "muster days" on military events, and "revolutionary days" on political developments. Sundays present the perfect opportunity to examine family life and religion of the time.

Historians had always known that roughly half the population of eighteenth-century Williamsburg was African-American, a few free, most enslaved. Until the 1970s, however, the only representatives of this half consisted of a few dozen housekeepers, custodians, and cooks who worked in costume in the exhibition buildings. The difficult topic of slavery had long been ignored, in part to avoid giving offense and in part because there was little in the way of historical information or artifacts to show the presence of slaves on the Williamsburg "stage" accurately.

"Enslaving Virginia" deals with the origins and development of Virginia's slave system. The reconstructed slave quarter at Carter's Grove helps provide an authentic setting.

One way to address slavery was to create that stage. Starting in 1987, the building tradesmen reconstructed the slave quarter at Carter's Grove plantation. Five years later, a service yard behind the Thomas Everard House began providing a place for visitors to learn about the servants and slaves who once worked on that property. In 1999, work began behind the Peyton Randolph House to reconstruct its two-story kitchen and other outbuildings on their original sites, an ideal setting

for presenting African-American life in eighteenth-century Williamsburg.

Another way to shed light on African-Americans, women, and all ranks of society in eighteenth-century Williamsburg was to use actors to personalize their stories. Colonial Williamsburg had flirted with "performance art" for many years before finally committing to a serious relationship. Half a dozen actors were hired and trained to assume the roles of real eighteenth-century people. The summer of 1979 provided many startling moments for unsuspecting visitors who happened on this entertaining and thought-provoking method of teaching history. A man locked in the pillory for drunkenness, a tavern slave snapping beans in the kitchen, a black Baptist preacher, a field hand tending tobacco plants—each actor perfected several roles and slipped in and out of them with apparent ease. As the summer progressed and the wrinkles in first-person technique smoothed out, even the skeptics came to accept the program. Character interpreters could address certain topics more effectively than could tour guides, static period rooms, or traditional interpretive techniques.

African-American programs proliferated during the 1980s. "African Traditions," an evening program, presented stories and music to the audience within the Historic Area. A black music program featured religious, secular, vocal, and instrumental selections typical of the period. "The Storyteller" examined the black oral legacy. A two-hour walking tour called "The Other Half" introduced visitors to the role of African-Americans in eighteenth-century Williamsburg, while "Behind Closed Doors" targeted schoolchildren for the same purpose. Supported by major corporate funding from AT&T in 1988, the programs were gathered together under the leadership of Rex Ellis into a new African-American Interpretation and Presentation Department where the planning, research, and implementation could be coordinated. The work culminated

Permanent and changing exhibits at the Wallace Museum showcase Colonial Williamsburg's vast collection of English and American decorative arts.

in 1999 with a yearlong emphasis on African-American history called "Enslaving Virginia."

The talented cast of the Company of Colonial Performers appeared in the Historic Area during the day as character interpreters and staged eighteenth-century plays at night. Some of these people of the past were anonymous: a lady on horseback dressed in fashionable riding habit or a merchant tending to business in the Greenhow Store. Others, such as George and Martha Washington or Patrick Henry, were instantly recognizable.

Period plays were not new to Williamsburg. After World War II, William and Mary students gave performances of eighteenth-century plays on the weekends for tourists and townspeople alike until the 1960s. In 1978, Colonial Williamsburg began producing its own plays at the Lodge Auditorium. New research buttressed the program. A reproduction play set designed in the London style was built. Efforts were made to present plays once produced in the colonies. More accurate wigs, costumes, and acting styles were developed. By the 1980s, the troupe was performing a variety of authentic pieces, from short comic plays to ballad operas, two nights a week.

Mini-performances were staged at less conventional sites throughout the Historic Area. A witch trial inside the Capitol's General Court room, the funeral of Lord Botetourt, or the festive arrival of Lady Dunmore are actual historical events brought to life outside the confines of traditional theater. Using actors and character interpreters permitted Colonial Williamsburg to deal with important subjects seldom discussed, such as death, mourning, slavery, and religion.

More women's history was explored and incorporated into the character interpreters' schedule. Topics like marriage, childbirth, and widowhood had places in the new plan. A successful program called "According to the Ladies" began in 1984 as a tour of Williamsburg from a feminine perspective. To strengthen the foundations for such programs, Colonial Williamsburg (with the College of William and Mary through the Omohundro Institute of Early American History and Culture) hosted the Conference on Women in Early America in 1981. In 1992, Colonial Williamsburg dedicated March to women's history and filled the month with special events, plays, character interpretation, and lectures.

A flurry of "new" old buildings entered the scene during the eighties. Bassett Hall's opening in 1980 was followed by the Public Hospital (1985), the last of Williamsburg's major public buildings to be reconstructed. A long-awaited decorative arts museum entered through the Public Hospital became reality that same year. Named for its benefactor, the DeWitt Wallace Museum provides at last a home for the thousands of treasures that could not be exhibited in Historic Area buildings. The Courthouse (which had been used for decades for ticket sales) opened as an exhibition building with regular reenactments of

colonial court cases. The stocks and pillories were moved from the Gaol to Market Square. A major archaeological excavation began behind the Peyton Randolph House in 1979 to learn enough about the outbuildings and domestic life there to reconstruct and reinterpret them. Using eighteenth-century tools and techniques, colonial tradesmen have begun slowly bringing the domestic yard back to its former appearance. In an early effort to improve accessibility, Colonial Williamsburg began installing wheelchair ramps in 1981 at unobtrusive entrances of exhibition buildings.

That same year, Historic Area stores took a shocking step into the present by accepting credit cards for the first time. Two years later, another general store brought to nine the number of eighteenth-century shops. Based on extensive research into store appearances and inventories, the John Greenhow Store re-created as far as possible the inventory of a general store of the period. The staff of the Greenhow Store actively interpreted eighteenth-century commerce with assistance from a series of actors who portrayed John Greenhow, his son, Robert, a sea captain, and various shoppers. The Ham Shop, the last modern store within the Historic Area, was returned to its colonial roots as M. Dubois Grocer.

Golf came to Colonial Williamsburg in 1947 with a 9-hole course behind the Inn. That course was entirely redesigned by Robert Trent Jones into the Golden Horseshoe, a challenging 18-hole course that opened in 1963. A 9-hole course, the Spotswood Executive, opened the next year. The game's increasing popularity led to a third course, the 18-hole Golden Horseshoe "Green," designed by architect Rees Jones in 1991.

In 1989, Shields Tavern opened near the Capitol building. The most authentic of the dining taverns, Shields offered an unusual treat for those curious about *real* eighteenth-century fare. Called the Shields Sampler, this popular selection gave diners a taste of several foods prepared from recipes found in period cookbooks. To enhance the eighteenth-century experience for guests staying in the Historic Area's Colonial Houses, a separate check-in area, the Orrell Kitchen, was established in 1997 and staffed by costumed employees.

The authenticity emphasis of the eighties saw some trades such as papermaking and stringed instrument making dropped because they were not practiced in Williamsburg during colonial times. More recently, carpenters, tailors, wigmakers, and various domestic tradespeople have come on board. With a training program to ensure that skills are passed along to future generations, apprentices work toward becoming journeymen, and journeymen labor to earn the coveted title of master craftsman.

Special projects caught the attention of the media. The first Colonial Fair Days, known today as Market Days, occurred in 1980. Carpenters erected wooden booths on Market Square to sell handcrafted baskets, baked goods, fresh vegetables, and beverages. Ever since

Schoolchildren across the country participate in Colonial Williamsburg's electronic field trips, interacting with people from the past in programs that mesh with the local curriculum.

1982, scores of imaginary fires have been doused with the help of the reproduction fire engine built by Williamsburg's tradesmen. A more authentic blacksmith shop was reconstructed on its original site by the housewrights and occupied with much fanfare in 1986 by smiths who "moved the fire" from the old Deane Forge site to the forge at the James Anderson Blacksmith Shop. The Colonial Nursery was established across from Bruton Parish Church in 1996. From March through December, costumed gardeners pursue their trade and sell historically accurate plants, seeds, holiday greenery, and reproduction gardening tools.

The Music Teacher's Shop closed. Music lessons and impromptu performances now take place throughout the Historic Area in homes where they would have occurred during colonial times. Today's music program, with its costumed people of the past, its evening walking tours, and its musical diversions at the Palace, Capitol, Courthouse, and other exhibition dwellings, gives the visitor a chance to experience different sorts of music, songs, and dance in appropriate settings.

For decades, Colonial Williamsburg has had a strong program for teachers, providing individual training, classroom materials, and lesson plans to elementary and secondary educators. Since 1988, the weeklong Teacher's Institute has provided more than 1,900 teachers with an in-depth look at Virginia history and an introduction to interactive teaching techniques.

Technology pulled the eighteenth century into the twenty-first. Although 130,000 schoolchildren visit the Historic Area every year on field trips, Colonial Williamsburg officials recognized that economic and geographic considerations would always prevent most of our nation's students from visiting in person. Colonial Williamsburg marched into the American classroom in 1996 with its innovative electronic field trips. Through the magic of satellite technology, the World Wide Web, and the telephone, students take numerous trips back in time each year, visiting with character interpreters and talking directly to them about subjects such as the Revolutionary War, African-American history, eighteenth-century religion, or the science of archaeology.

Much remains to be accomplished in the years ahead, and the Colonial Williamsburg Foundation is well positioned to support the creation of new endeavors with the Bruton Heights School Education Center, completed in 1997. First conceived by Colonial Williamsburg's fifth president, Charles Longsworth, as a place to consolidate Historic Area support operations, this campuslike facility houses the modern John D. Rockefeller, Jr. Library (a research library specializing in the history and culture of the colonial Chesapeake), the DeWitt Wallace Collections and Conservation Building with state-of-the-art storage and conservation facilities, laboratories for audiovisual productions, costume research and fabrication facilities, offices for architects, research historians, archaeologists, and architectural historians, and classrooms for training. If the Historic Area is the heart of Colonial Williamsburg, surely the Bruton Heights complex is the brain.

The Bruton Heights School Education Center today. The Rockefellers financially backed the original Bruton Heights School (*top*) when it opened in 1940 as a model school for black students. The building also served as the local African-American community center.

Williamsburg® PRODUCTS PROGRAM

When the job of restoring a building moved indoors, those trying to re-create historically accurate settings quickly discovered the limitations of antiques. Often the right kind or the right quality did not exist at any price or, if it did, not in the quantity needed. To locate one or even two appropriate Virginia-made walnut side chairs of the correct period might be possible, to find a dozen matching chairs was not. Thus the Reproductions Program was born.

At a meeting in New York in 1930, John D. Rockefeller, Jr., and several of his staff discussed refurbishing the Raleigh Tavern as a working inn. It was reported that the furniture would be period reproductions but the silverware, glasses, and china could not since none was available in the marketplace. But Rockefeller would not compromise with authenticity. He authorized Wedgwood & Sons in England to reproduce china from the fragments of queensware excavated on the Raleigh Tavern site. Then, as such china was unavailable to the public, he suggested that "the purposes of education might be furthered by the sale of this ware."

Rockefeller was also influenced by the public's eagerness to acquire reproductions. The Colonial Williamsburg experiment had caught the country's imagination in a profound way and it soon became apparent that the "Williamsburg look" was more than the latest fad. Architects, interior designers, and decorators pleaded for the opportunity to use the colors, designs, and materials they saw in the Historic Area. Manufacturers were selected and authorized to reproduce china, silverware, glass, furniture, prints, fabrics, and lighting fixtures from the antiques and designs in the Colonial Williamsburg collection. By 1937, a place to sell them had been built next to the new Williamsburg Inn. The Craft House, as it was called, shared space with the original Reception Center for many years.

Today, Colonial Williamsburg operates one of the best loved and most successful products programs in the country, recently launching an exciting new collection of home furnishings called Williamsburg Pure. Simple. Today. Inspired by the tradition of fine craftsmanship and the origin of American style, the collection lends a contemporary voice to Williamsburg design with a fresh, casual aesthetic perfect for today's lifestyles.

Over the last seventy-five years, the Williamsburg Products Program has grown significantly, currently managing more than sixty manufacturers who produce high-quality furniture and decorative ware available in Colonial Williamsburg and in stores across the United States.

THE WINDOWS OF WILLIAMSBURG

"Through which men may look down the vistas of the past"

Anniversaries are milestones for measuring the distance traveled and for contemplating the journey ahead. During the past seventy-five years, Colonial Williamsburg has come farther along the road to restoration and interpretation than its founders ever imagined, yet the pavement still stretches into the horizon. Colonial Williamsburg's seventh president, Colin Campbell, calls it "a perpetual exercise in historic preservation." Much remains to be done and much will be accomplished in the busy years ahead.

As the twenty-first century opens, the greatest physical challenge facing Colonial Williamsburg is conserving its great collection of buildings. The oldest original buildings are passing their three hundredth birthdays. Reconstructions such as the Capitol and the Governor's Palace have endured sixty-seven years of wear and tear from tens of millions of feet. Work is underway at Bassett Hall to repair a leaky cellar and replace the roof in anticipation of reopening in 2002. Renovation recently was completed at Wetherburn's Tavern and significant work is planned for the Lightfoot House, the brick Georgian mansion on Francis Street used for distinguished visitors and heads of state.

New building continues. Behind the Peyton Randolph House, the two-story kitchen was reconstructed on its original site in 2001; the other outbuildings will be completed over the next few years. Design drawings are being made for the eventual reconstruction of the coffeehouse near the Capitol, and a colonial theater site is being excavated in hopes that it, too, can be brought back to life.

Visitor facilities—hotels, restaurants, shops, and information centers—are receiving considerable attention. Massive renovations at the Williamsburg Inn are nearly complete. A new Woodlands hotel has emerged adjacent to the Visitor Center, and major upgrading is contemplated for the Williamsburg Lodge. Merchants Square, one of America's first planned shopping districts, is exploring revitalization and expansion opportunities. The Visitor Center is being modernized and enlarged and will offer an orientation experience par excellence. A new family restaurant, an expanded bookstore, a learning resource center for teachers, and a pedestrian promenade add to the visitor's experience.

A renovated guest room at the Williamsburg Inn.

Working together, Colonial Williamsburg and the College of William and Mary are ushering in the third millennium with two ambitious theater projects. This commitment to the lively arts is a fitting way to recognize Williamsburg as the location of the first theater in the British colonies. The college is working on a new design for the Lake Matoaka amphitheater (where the popular outdoor drama *The Common Glory* was staged from 1947 to 1976) while Colonial Williamsburg finishes the new, enlarged Kimball Theater in Merchants Square as a permanent home for its eighteenth-century theater program. The two theaters will serve students, tourists, and residents of Williamsburg.

Town-and-gown cooperation spearheaded by William and Mary president Tim Sullivan and senior vice president Rick Nahm, who was acting president of Colonial Williamsburg for nine months, includes the revitalization of Merchants Square. This shopping district was established in 1932 at the foot of the college triangle and assumed an important role as the retail heart of Williamsburg. The William and Mary Bookstore (a Barnes & Noble enterprise now located in the space formerly occupied by Casey's Department Store) and the Kimball Theater are the first achievements of this initiative.

The generosity of one person began Colonial Williamsburg; the generosity of thousands of people carries it on. From the start, donors played a vital role in Williamsburg's mission. Admirers of Colonial Williamsburg made spontaneous gifts of antiques and cash over the years, but no organized fund-raising program existed during the organization's first half-century.

Colonial Williamsburg's fiftieth anniversary celebration, which coincided with the American Bicentennial, launched a new era. "From then on," says Colin Campbell, "America at large began to participate in the work Mr. Rockefeller began. In 1976, the Foundation opened a development office, its first organized effort to invite all of Colonial Williamsburg's admirers to associate themselves with Mr. Rockefeller's undertaking; to help preserve the prize he provided for his country; to join in supporting the institution he left to the nation. And the response has been extraordinary."

Through the generosity of donors large and small, America's investment in Colonial Williamsburg has grown ever stronger. The total of gifts made that first year of 1976 amounted to $50,000 from about 540 donors. A quarter-century later, the millennium went out with a flourish: 88,000 donors generously contributed $46.8 million, making 2000 the most successful fund-raising year ever.

Although John D. Rockefeller, Jr., died in 1960, his family continued to share his interest in the Foundation, and over the years, his sons and many of his grandchildren and great-grandchildren generously contributed their time and their money. All five Rockefeller sons were involved with Colonial Williamsburg, in particular Winthrop and John D. 3rd. Among the grandchildren, Abby O'Neill served as a trustee for twenty-eight years (as did her husband, George O'Neill), retiring as vice chairman of the board of trustees in 1994. Steven C. Rockefeller served as a trustee during the 1990s and Mrs. John D. (Sharon Percy) Rockefeller IV joined the board in 2001.

A conservator restores an antique chair.

Second only to the Rockefeller family in their support of Colonial Williamsburg were Lila and DeWitt Wallace, founders of *Reader's Digest* Association, whose long love affair with Williamsburg caused them to underwrite the reconstruction of the Public Hospital, a modern collections and conservation building at the Bruton Heights complex, and the magnificent decorative arts museum completed in 1985. They established the DeWitt Wallace Fund for Colonial Williamsburg, which continues to support the DeWitt Wallace Museum,

ABBY ALDRICH ROCKEFELLER FOLK ART MUSEUM

The first property purchased by Dr. Goodwin for Mr. Rockefeller, the Paradise House was among the first buildings restored to its eighteenth-century appearance. Early in 1935, its doors were opened to the public. Visitors to the Paradise House did not walk through rooms furnished with period antiques, however. Instead, they saw examples of American folk art collected over the previous decade by Abby Aldrich Rockefeller. She had been one of the first Americans to appreciate the value of "primitive" folk art: the paintings, sculptures, and household furnishings created by untrained artists and craftspeople working outside academic art. Her loan soon became a gift and the gift became the nucleus of the Abby Aldrich Rockefeller Folk Art Museum, built in her memory by her husband in 1957. It was greatly enlarged to provide additional exhibition space for the growing collection in 1991.

collections and conservation, and outreach education every year. Walter Annenberg's extraordinary generosity brought many benefits, including a magnificent gift that was applied to the Bruton Heights School Education Center. June and Joe Hennage have committed their home and antique collection to Colonial Williamsburg. Bill and Gretchen Kimballs' recent "Young Patriots Fund" is surely the largest commitment to youth history education in the nation.

In recent years, a number of nationally known collectors have followed in the steps of Abby Aldrich Rockefeller and donated or funded important collections of art and antiques to Colonial Williamsburg. They include Elizabeth and Miodrag Blagojevich, C. H. Carter, Alma and Harry Coon, Mary Jewett Gaiser, Cora Ginsburg, June and Joe Hennage, John Hyman, Lowry Dale Kirby, Ruth and Joe Lasser, Foster and Muriel McCarl, Tasha Tudor, Anna Glen Vietor, and Jimmy and Henry Weldon.

Monetary gifts have been responsible for hundreds of important milestones including Carter's Grove plantation and the Country Road that links it to Williamsburg, the restoration of the Courthouse, the presence of Thomas Jefferson and other character interpreters, the new stable complex, the St. George Tucker House restoration, the folk art, archaeology, and decorative arts museums, the reconstruction of the Peyton Randolph outbuildings, the theater renovations at Merchants Square, Bruton Heights School Education Center, and the Fife and Drum building. In 1979, a special donor group named the Raleigh Tavern Society began with two dozen charter members. Today, its 300 members are a remarkably generous group whose aggregate contributions support vital educational activities.

Committed as he is to Historic Area improvements and programs, President Campbell is keenly focused on exporting Colonial Williamsburg to the millions of Americans as yet unfamiliar with its educational mission and patriotic message. "We have more to convey than the classic historical message of how and why revolution came to America. We in Williamsburg have the opportunity to deal with the critical issues of the past that continue to dominate our present—questions of race, religion, gender, civics, and participation in the political process—and in doing so, make a significant contribution to America's future. Colonial Williamsburg is not only about yesterday. It is about the impact of yesterday on today and on tomorrow."

You can almost hear the minister and the philanthropist applaud.

EPILOGUE

The United States of America didn't begin as much as it evolved. Much of that evolutionary process took place in and around Williamsburg. The oldest representative assembly in the New World, the grand ideals of 1776, the construction of a unique American culture by the people of three continents, the saga of westward expansion, the roots of American entrepreneurship and international consumerism—Williamsburg is the story of how we became Americans. Colonial Williamsburg is the time machine that enables the past to speak to the present.

During Colonial Williamsburg's seventy-five-year history, people changed, leaders changed, programs changed. Furnishings, landscape, and even the colors of the buildings changed. But the fundamental ideals never budged. The commitment to authenticity and to an honest portrayal of our nation's history remains rock solid. The belief that future generations will grow stronger by learning the lessons from history has guided the work of the Colonial Williamsburg Foundation through depressions, wars, social upheavals, and controversy. The possibilities of Colonial Williamsburg first grasped by Dr. W. A. R. Goodwin and understood so well by John D. Rockefeller, Jr., have succeeded beyond their hopes and expectations. The minister's prophecy has come true: "There will be windows built here, through which men may look down the vistas of the past." May the windows of Williamsburg always be open.

COLONIAL WILLIAMSBURG FOUNDATION BOARD OF TRUSTEES 2001

COLONIAL WILLIAMSBURG COMPANY BOARD OF DIRECTORS 2001

Colin G. Campbell
Chairman
Colonial Williamsburg Company
Williamsburg, Virginia

Jeanne B. Daniel
Retail Consultant
New Canaan, Connecticut

Joshua P. Darden, Jr.
President
Darden Properties, Inc.
Norfolk, Virginia

Edward S. Dunn, Jr.
President
Colonial Williamsburg Company
Williamsburg, Virginia

Clayton W. Frye, Jr.
Sr. Associate of
Laurance S. Rockefeller
New York, New York

Michael F. Glennie
Sr. Vice President
Boca Resorts, Inc.
Boca Raton, Florida

Gordon F. Rainey, Jr.
Partner and Chairman of the
Executive Committee
Hunton & Williams
Richmond, Virginia

Robert M. Solmson
Chairman and CEO
RFS Hotel Investors, Inc.
Memphis, Tennessee

Richard G. Tilghman
Chairman-Retired
SunTrust Bank, Mid-Atlantic
Richmond, Virginia

COLONIAL WILLIAMSBURG FOUNDATION ADMINISTRATIVE OFFICERS 2001

Colin G. Campbell
Chairman, President, and CEO

Edward S. Dunn, Jr.
Senior Vice President–Colonial Williamsburg Foundation and President–Colonial Williamsburg Company

Robert B. Taylor
Senior Vice President–Finance and Administration

John S. Bacon
Vice President, Secretary, and General Counsel

Cary Carson
Vice President–Research

Charles K. Driscoll
Vice President–Strategic Projects

Rex M. Ellis
Vice President–Historic Area

John T. Hallowell
Vice President–Colonial Williamsburg Foundation and President–Hospitality Colonial Williamsburg Company

Christine R. Hoek
Vice President–Advancement

Andrew J. Hungerman III
Vice President–Operations

Ronald L. Hurst
Vice President–Collections and Museums and Chief Curator

Janet D. Kane
Vice President–Products

Richard L. McCluney, Jr.
Vice President–Productions, Publications, and Learning Ventures

Beatrix T. Rumford
Vice President–Special Projects

Katherine H. Whitehead
Vice President–Finance

COLONIAL WILLIAMSBURG LEADERSHIP

PRESIDENTS

Vernon M. Geddy, Sr. (February–April, 1928)

Arthur Woods (1928–1935)

Kenneth Chorley (1935–1958)

Carlisle H. Humelsine (1958–1977)

Charles R. Longsworth (1977–1992)

Robert C. Wilburn (1992–1999)

Colin G. Campbell (2000–)

CHAIRMEN OF THE BOARD OF TRUSTEES

Arthur Woods (1935–1939)

John D. Rockefeller 3rd (1939–1953)

Winthrop Rockefeller (1953–1973)

Lewis F. Powell, Jr. (1973–1977)

Carlisle H. Humelsine (1977–1985)

Charles L. Brown (1985–1991)

Charles R. Longsworth (1991–1994)

George B. Beitzel (1994–1998)

Colin G. Campbell (1998–)

"That the future may learn from the past"

DR. GOODWIN'S DREAM

"If you have ever walked around Williamsburg late on a moonlight night, when most of the people who now live here are fast asleep, and felt the presence and companionship of the people who used to live here in the long gone years, and remembered the things that they did and the things that they stood for, and pictured them going into or coming out of the old houses in which they once lived, and remembered the things which they said in the House of Burgesses and at the old College—you would then know what an interesting place Williamsburg is. You would realize that it is about the most interesting place in America.

There are thousands of cities in this country with Main Streets, but only one with a Duke of Gloucester Street like ours. There are many Protestant Churches, but none so long conspicuously in use as Bruton Parish . . . when you walk around Williamsburg late on a moonlight night you can see the Indians on the Court Green, where they used to meet to make their treaties of peace . . . and you can see the agents of old Lord Dunmore, stealing the powder out of the Powder Horn, and you can hear the rattle of the horses' hoofs coming down the Richmond Road as Patrick Henry and the Hanover Volunteers ride on to Williamsburg and demand the powder be restored."

Third printing, 2007
Printed in China

DR. GOODWIN'S DREAM

"If you have ever walked around Williamsburg late on a moonlight night, when most of the people who now live here are fast asleep, and felt the presence and companionship of the people who used to live here in the long gone years, and remembered the things that they did and the things that they stood for, and pictured them going into or coming out of the old houses in which they once lived, and remembered the things which they said in the House of Burgesses and at the old College—you would then know what an interesting place Williamsburg is. You would realize that it is about the most interesting place in America.

There are thousands of cities in this country with Main Streets, but only one with a Duke of Gloucester Street like ours. There are many Protestant Churches, but none so long conspicuously in use as Bruton Parish . . . when you walk around Williamsburg late on a moonlight night you can see the Indians on the Court Green, where they used to meet to make their treaties of peace . . . and you can see the agents of old Lord Dunmore, stealing the powder out of the Powder Horn, and you can hear the rattle of the horses' hoofs coming down the Richmond Road as Patrick Henry and the Hanover Volunteers ride on to Williamsburg and demand the powder be restored."

Third printing, 2007
Printed in China